essentials
EGG

essentials
EGG

Exploit the versatility, aroma, and taste

Edited by Jane Donovan

CB
CONTEMPORARY BOOKS

With much love to Gary Connell and thanks for his culinary inspiration

A QUINTET BOOK

Published in the United States in 1999 by
Contemporary Books
A division of NTC/Contemporary Publishing Group, Inc.
4255 West Touhy Avenue
Lincolnwood (Chicago), Illinois 60712-1975 U.S.A.

ISBN 0-8092-2326-0

This book was designed and produced by
Quintet Publishing Limited
6 Blundell Street
London N7 9BH

Creative Director: Richard Dewing
Art Director: Paula Marchant
Designer: Isobel Gillan
Senior Editor: Clare Hubbard
Assistant Editor: Carine Tracanelli
Editor: Jane Donovan

Typeset in Great Britain by
Central Southern Typesetters, Eastbourne
Manufactured in Hong Kong by
Regent Publishing Services Ltd
Printed in China by
Leefung-Asco Printers Ltd

Library of Congress cataloging-in-publication data is available from the
United States Library of Congress.

Material in this book has previously appeared in Quintet titles.

Note

Because of the risk of salmonella poisoning, raw eggs should not be served to babies and young children, the ill or elderly, or to pregnant women. Cooking eggs will eliminate the risk of salmonella poisoning, but as drinks use raw eggs, the above considerations must be heeded during preparation. Eggs have a high cholesterol content, and should also be avoided by those on a cholesterol-free diet or with limited cholesterol intake. Always use fresh, unblemished eggs and ensure that no shell particles are accidentally included in drinks.

Fresh herbs should be used in the recipes unless otherwise stated.
If using an ice-cream machine always refer to the manufacturer's instructions regarding capacity and operation.

Titles also available in this series are *Chocolate* (ISBN 0-8092-2328-7) and *Tomato* (ISBN 0-8092-2327-9).

CONTENTS

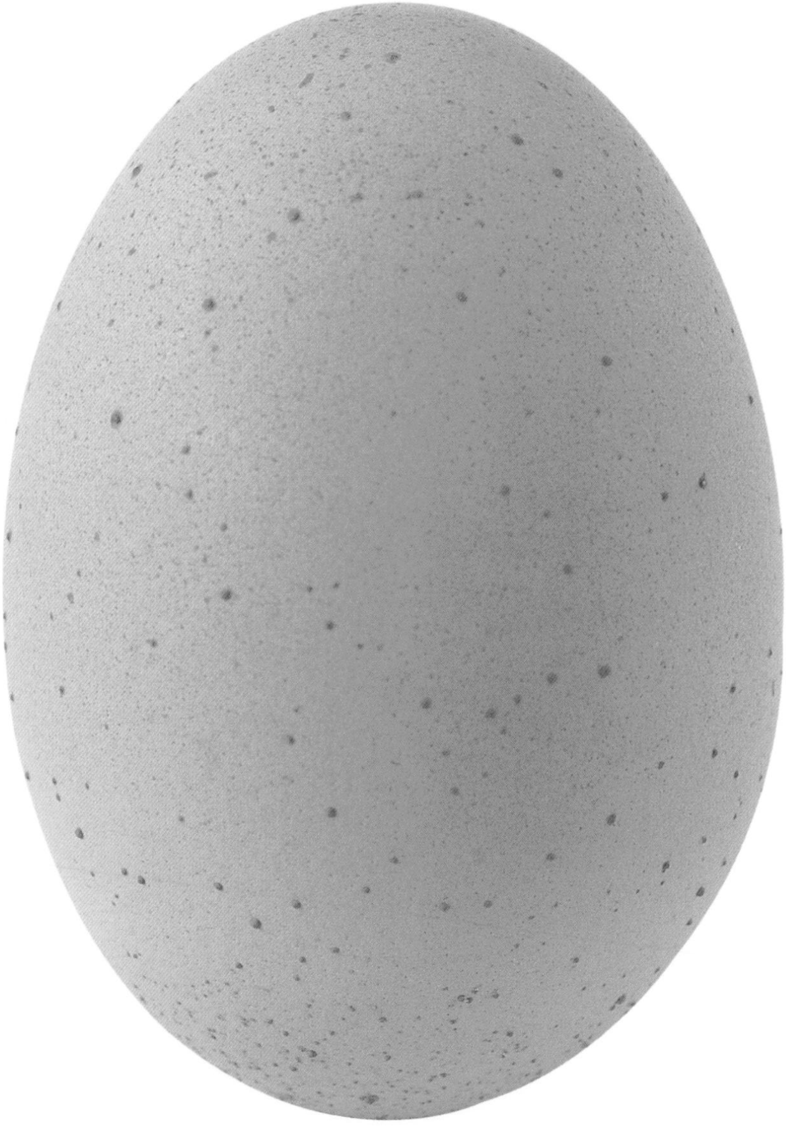

Introduction

eggs are full of nutrients, proteins, vitamins, and minerals. They are also an **essential** stand-by ingredient and can be used to make many quick dishes including omelets, soufflés, and classic eggs en cocotte (eggs **baked** in buttered ramekin dishes). Eggs can be cooked in a variety of ways, from scrambling to frying. Store good-quality mayonnaise, an egg-based product, in a cool place, along with a carton of fresh eggs. It makes a useful basis for an instant **aïoli** dip with crisp, raw vegetables, or try swirling mayonnaise on rounds of toasted French bread as an accompaniment to fish soup.

Many recipes call for **eggs** at room temperature so they are better stored in a cool place, where they will remain in good shape for two weeks. If you have no other alternative, place your eggs in the lowest part of the refrigerator (near the freezing compartment is usually too cold). Remove them a few hours in advance of **cooking** to allow them to come to room temperature. This will help to keep them from breaking when you boil them and curdling in cake recipes. Store eggs thin end down and away from strong smells because the shells are porous and they can absorb other food flavors.

Finally, while deliciously **versatile,** eggs require careful cooking. Some eggs have been shown to contain salmonella so the elderly, young, babies, pregnant women, and people with poor immune defense systems are advised not to eat raw or lightly cooked eggs (see page 4 for further information).

The flavors of eggs

Brown or white, eggs can be enjoyed on their own and they play a vital role in many recipes. The best-flavored eggs are fresh free-range farm eggs with their richly-colored yolks. Eggs come in extra large, large, medium, and small sizes, and most recipes call for medium eggs. Bring eggs to room temperature prior to cooking for the best results. Shown here are some of the most popular eggs:

1

1 brown eggs are no different from the white variety, however they are more aesthetically pleasing.

₂free-range eggs—of course, the ultimate free-range eggs are the ones that you purchase direct from farms, where the hens run free.

duck eggs vary the flavor of your cooking.

₃quail eggs are available from most supermarkets and delicatessens. These are great hard-cooked in salads.

₄fresh hen eggs in a variety of sizes are used in most recipes.

Specialist **egg** products

Egg-based products are widely available in delicatessens and supermarkets. They are essential items in any kitchen and can be used to enliven all kinds of dishes. Use these products as a stand-by and you will quickly be able to make a whole range of different sauces, soup garnishes, salads, and appetizers, and create instant snacks as well as main courses. Shown here are some useful egg-based ingredients:

2

hollandaise sauce can be served with hard-cooked eggs and steamed asparagus for a light appetizer.

₁**mayonnaise**–always use the best quality. Try adding different flavors or fresh herbs, such as snipped chives, parsley, or garlic, to plain mayonnaise.

béarnaise sauce is traditionally served with filet mignon.

béchamel sauce is often the basis of lasagne and other pasta recipes, and many fish dishes.

₂**caesar sauce** is the classic salad dressing.

₃**thousand island dressing** is used for salads or as a sandwich spread.

Cooking Techniques

Eggs can be cooked in a number of different ways and many of the methods described below are used in the recipes in this book. These are the basic techniques to get you started. (Refer to page 4 for advice on health and safety.)

Boiled Eggs

For soft-cooked eggs, choose a heavy saucepan that is small enough to prevent the eggs from dancing about and cracking while cooking. Bring some water to a boil, then reduce to a gentle simmer. With a tablespoon, lower the eggs carefully into the water. Simmer for 1 minute, then remove the saucepan from the heat. Add the lid and leave the eggs for a further 5 to 6 minutes depending on size. The white will be just set and the yolk will be soft and creamy. Experiment with really fresh eggs (less than four days old) as these will require a slightly longer cooking time.

For hard-cooked eggs, place the eggs in a small heavy saucepan of cold water. Allow to simmer for 6 to 7 minutes depending on the size of the eggs. (The yolks will be hard but the centers will still have a nice creamy consistency.) Cool under cold running water to prevent the eggs from cooking any more. Tap gently to crack the surface of the eggs, peel away the shells, and rinse under cold running water to remove any traces of shell before serving.

Poached Eggs

Use really fresh eggs for this method of cooking. Fill a small skillet with water to a depth of $1\frac{1}{2}$ inches. Turn on the heat and bring the water to barely simmering. Break each egg gently into a cup and then pour into the water. Unless you are an experienced hand, don't attempt to poach more than two at a time. Three minutes is just right for larger eggs, or according to taste. While the eggs are cooking, you can help the process along by basting the tops with water.

   Use a slotted spoon to remove the eggs from the skillet and transfer to paper towels to remove the excess water. (Remember to remove the eggs in the same order they were placed into the pan, for even cooking times.)

Scrambled Eggs

Beat two large eggs and season them with salt and pepper. Place a small piece of butter in a heavy saucepan over a gentle heat and swirl it around to coat the base of the saucepan thoroughly. When the butter is foaming, add the beaten eggs, and stir the mixture constantly with a wooden spoon, working the spoon into the corners of the saucepan to prevent the egg sticking.

  While the egg is still slightly liquid, remove the saucepan from the heat, and add another piece of butter to give the eggs a creamy texture and keep stirring. The cooking process can be finished with the heat of the saucepan.

Frying Eggs

Heat some oil or fat in a large skillet until hot, but not smoking. Carefully crack the egg into a cup and then pour into the skillet and it will start to set. If liked, baste the egg with the oil or fat, and serve sunny side up when the egg is cooked to your liking.

Beating Egg Whites

Once egg whites are over-beaten they start to collapse. Whisking incorporates air, but too much air causes the foam bubbles to burst. The eggs are ready when you lift the whisk up and they stand in soft, white peaks. If you are folding eggs into another mixture, perhaps in a mousse or soufflé, fold in one metal tablespoon of beaten egg first, then fold in the rest.

Separating Eggs

Some recipes call for just the whites or the yolks of eggs, and some require both, but at different times. To separate eggs, take two bowls and place them side by side. Crack an egg carefully against the side of one of the bowls. Immediately begin to drain off the white from the egg, transferring the yolk across from shell to shell until the white is drained from the shells. Then place the egg yolk in a separate bowl. Practice makes perfect!

THE BASICS

Ham, Chicory, & Egg Gratin

This delicious recipe can be served as a light appetizer or supper dish.

SERVES 2

4 chicory heads, quartered

1 Tbsp lemon juice

4 hard-cooked eggs, shelled and sliced (see page 12)

4 slices ham, diced

2 large tomatoes, sliced

1 to 2 tsp wholegrain mustard

1¼ cups prepared cheese sauce

2 Tbsp shredded Cheddar cheese

● Preheat the oven to 375°F. Blanch the chicory in boiling water with the lemon juice for 5 minutes; drain.

● Place the chicory in a gratin dish with the eggs, ham, and tomatoes. Beat the mustard into the cheese sauce. Pour the sauce over the gratin mixture, sprinkle with cheese, and bake for 25 minutes.

Cheese Sauce

If you can't find this sauce in your local store it can be made quickly.

2 Tbsp butter or margarine

¼ cup all-purpose flour

2½ cups warm milk

1 tsp Dijon mustard

1½ cups shredded mature Cheddar cheese

Salt and freshly ground black pepper

Melt the butter or margarine in a medium-sized saucepan, and stir in the flour. Cook for 30 seconds, then remove from the heat.

Stir in the milk, a little at a time, blending after each addition to prevent lumps. Return sauce to a medium heat, and stir until the sauce thickens and boils.

Add the mustard and cheese, and season to taste with salt and freshly ground black pepper. Continue to cook, stirring constantly, until the cheese has melted.

Eggs Benedict

Served with the famous French Hollandaise Sauce, this is a breakfast or brunch classic. The sauce also goes especially well with steamed vegetables, such as asparagus or artichokes.

SERVES **2** TO **4**

4 medium eggs (see page 4)

⅓ to ⅔ quantity Hollandaise Sauce
 (see page 19)

4 muffins or thick slices white bread

4 slices ham

2 tomatoes, sliced

1 Tbsp chopped parsley

● Lightly poach the eggs (see page 13) and warm the Hollandaise Sauce. Toast the muffins or bread, fold each slice of ham in half, and place on top. Cover with the tomatoes. Place the eggs on top, spoon over the sauce, sprinkle with parsley, and serve.

Hollandaise Sauce

This rich, creamy sauce is delicious served with salmon or asparagus.

SERVES **6**

2 Tbsp white wine vinegar

3 Tbsp water

I slice onion

I pinch ground mace

½ small bay leaf

6 black peppercorns

I Tbsp water

3 egg yolks (see page 4)

I½ sticks unsalted butter, at room temperature

Lemon juice, to taste

Salt and ground black pepper

● Place the first six ingredients in a small heavy saucepan and let simmer gently (uncovered) until the mixture is reduced to about I tablespoon. Strain the reduced mixture into a heatproof bowl, add I more tablespoon water, and season. Whisk in the egg yolks.

● Place the bowl over a heavy saucepan of barely simmering water, add I tablespoon of the butter, whisking until it has melted and the mixture has slightly thickened. Continue adding the butter I tablespoon at a time. Allow the butter to melt and the mixture to thicken before adding the next piece of butter.

● When all the butter has been added, continue whisking and cooking the sauce gently for a further 2 minutes. Remove the bowl, taste, and add lemon juice and seasoning as desired.

Country Eggs

This quick and easy-to-make recipe is a filling and tasty dish for brunch or a lunchtime snack.

SERVES **2**

8 oz waxy potatoes, diced

8 oz bacon, chopped

1 onion, chopped

2 Tbsp olive oil

⅛ stick butter

Salt and ground black pepper

4 medium eggs

1 Tbsp chopped parsley or chives

● Boil the potatoes for 5 minutes; drain and reserve. Sauté the bacon and onion in a large skillet for 5 minutes, then add the oil, butter, and potatoes. Cook for 10 minutes, stirring occasionally. Season to taste, add the eggs, and cook for 5 minutes until set. Sprinkle with herbs and serve.

Pipérade

This is a Mediterranean version of scrambled eggs that is served with fresh crusty bread.

SERVES **2** TO **3**

2 Tbsp olive oil

1 onion, chopped

2 garlic cloves, crushed

1 red, 1 yellow, and 1 green bell pepper,
    seeded and sliced

6 medium eggs

Salt and ground black pepper

2 Tbsp water

3 tomatoes, chopped

2 Tbsp chopped basil

Crusty bread, to serve

● Heat the oil in a large skillet and sauté the onion, garlic, and peppers for 10 minutes until soft. Beat the eggs with the seasoning and 2 tablespoons water, and add to the skillet with the tomatoes. Cook, stirring, until almost set. Sprinkle over the basil. Serve with crusty bread.

Spinach Roulade

A light and delicate dish that makes an impressive appetizer.

SERVES **4**

6 oz chopped spinach
¼ stick butter
Salt and ground black pepper
3 Tbsp shredded Cheddar cheese
4 eggs, separated (see page 15)
8 oz cream cheese
6 scallions, chopped
6 oz peeled shrimp, cooked and chopped

● Preheat the oven to 375°F. Wilt the spinach in butter for 3 minutes. Remove from heat. Add the seasoning, Cheddar cheese, and the egg yolks. Whisk the egg whites until stiff, then fold them into the mixture. Pour the mixture into a parchment-lined jelly-roll pan and bake for 10 minutes until set.

● Turn the roulade out of the pan and onto a serving plate. Remove the parchment. In a large bowl, blend the remaining ingredients and spread the mixture evenly over the surface of the roulade. Roll up the roulade and serve immediately.

Cajun Deviled Eggs

The tasso gives these deviled eggs their spicy taste. If you don't have tasso, use another ham, but add cayenne pepper and paprika to give it a Cajun flavor.

SERVES **3 TO 6**

6 hard-cooked eggs (see page 12)
¼ cup finely chopped tasso
1 Tbsp finely chopped green bell pepper
1 scallion, finely chopped
½ tsp lemon juice
2 Tbsp mayonnaise
2 Tbsp Dijon mustard
Pinch of freshly ground black pepper
Dash of hot pepper sauce

● Cut the eggs in half lengthwise. Remove the yolks, and put them in a small bowl. Set the whites aside. Mash the yolks with a fork. Add the remaining ingredients to the yolks, and mix well with a fork. Taste and adjust the seasonings. Spoon the mixture into the egg whites.

Egg & Garlic Fried Bread

This is a variation on French toast. The oil must be very hot so that the egg is sealed immediately (watch for a wavy look on the base of the skillet).

SERVES **3**

3 eggs
Few drops of warm water
2 Tbsp garlic, crushed
Salt and ground black pepper
3 Tbsp olive oil
6 slices of bread

● Beat the eggs in a bowl with a few drops of warm water. Add the crushed garlic and seasoning to the egg and mix well.

● Heat the oil in a large skillet. Dip the bread in the egg mixture so that both sides are covered, and place in the skillet. Fry on both sides until golden brown (the bread must be turned quickly to prevent the garlic from burning).

Scrambled Eggs with Smoked Salmon

This dish is often served with Buck's Fizz. Fill champagne flutes to about one-third with freshly squeezed orange juice, then top with chilled champagne.

SERVES **2** TO **4**

¼ stick butter

4 medium eggs

3 Tbsp light cream

Salt and ground black pepper

4 oz smoked salmon

2 Tbsp snipped chives

4 slices buttered toast, to serve

Ideas for Scrambled Egg Mixes

- *Any smoked fish, such as cooked smoked trout or mackerel, can be used instead of salmon.*
- *Use milk instead of cream for a lighter meal.*
- *Add a tablespoon of freshly chopped scallions to the eggs in place of herbs and salmon.*
- *Replace the salmon and chives with a mixture of wild mushrooms and freshly chopped thyme.*
- *Or try honey-roasted ham and small pieces of Swiss cheese.*

● Melt the butter in a small heavy saucepan. Beat the eggs with the cream and seasoning, and pour into the saucepan. Cook, stirring, for 2 minutes.

● Cut the salmon into thin strips and add it to the saucepan with the chives, stirring. Cook for approximately 2 minutes, depending on how you like your eggs. Serve with buttered toast.

PARTY PIECES

Chicken in Batter with Honey & Mustard

Try the great combination of chicken and honey in this delicious finger food.

SERVES **4** TO **6**

3 chicken breasts, diced into 1-in cubes

Salt and ground black pepper

2 eggs

Flour, to coat

4 Tbsp olive oil

8 Tbsp runny honey

1 tsp French mustard

1 tsp soy sauce

Place the chicken pieces in a large bowl. Season and break the eggs over the chicken pieces. Work the egg thoroughly into the chicken, using your hands. Add enough flour to make a thick coating over the chicken. The mixture should be of a consistency where it stops just short of dripping.

Heat the oil in a large skillet and fry the chicken until golden, turning frequently, for about 15 minutes. Remove the chicken from the heat and season.

In a bowl, blend the honey with the mustard and soy sauce. Drizzle the mixture over the chicken and serve immediately.

Paella Croquettes

A variation on the traditional Spanish dish. The croquettes can be made in advance and reheated in a microwave.

SERVES **4** TO **6**

1 lb risotto rice
1 medium onion, roughly chopped
1 bay leaf
1 tsp garlic, crushed
1 chicken broth cube
1 Tbsp olive oil
2 tsp turmeric

2 times the quantity of hot water or
    chicken broth to rice
10 oz chorizo sausage and smoked ham,
    mixed together in equal quantities
Seasoned flour
Bread crumbs
Egg wash (2 eggs, beaten with a little milk)
Oil, for frying
Chopped parsley, to serve

● Put the rice in a heavy saucepan and add the onion, bay leaf, garlic, broth cube, olive oil, and turmeric. Pour the hot water or chicken broth over the mixture. Place the saucepan over the heat and bring the mixture to a boil. Reduce the heat and simmer until the rice is soft and has absorbed all the water (about 15 minutes). Remove from the heat and let cool.

● Mince the meat in a food processor and add to the cold rice, mixing it in well. (There should be an equal ratio of rice to meat in the balls.) The mixture should be slightly moist, but easy to form into small balls. If your mixture is too wet, add a little flour or bread crumbs. Form the mixture into evenly sized balls and roll them in flour until lightly covered.

● Roll the balls in the egg wash and then in the bread crumbs. At this stage the croquettes may be refrigerated and kept until the next day, if preferred. Deep-fry in hot oil (365°F) until golden and crispy on the outside. Sprinkle with parsley and serve immediately.

Shredded Crêpes

Make as many crêpes as you like to use as a garnish. They are an original way to add texture and flavor to soups.

1 cup all-purpose flour

3 eggs

¼ cup vegetable oil, plus extra for frying

2 Tbsp herbs, chopped fine

● Beat the flour, eggs, and vegetable oil together in a bowl to make a smooth batter. Let stand for 30 to 60 minutes, then add the herbs.

● Heat some oil in a large skillet and, when smoking, pour in enough batter to cover the base of the skillet. Use a fish slice to keep scraping away at the edges of the crêpe and turn after about 1 minute. Fry on both sides until golden brown. Let cool and stack between layers of waxed paper.

● Tightly roll up a couple of crêpes. With a sharp knife, finely slice the crêpe to form thin shreds. Warm in the oven before using as a garnish.

Chopped Egg Garni

This pretty garnish is invaluable for all kinds of dishes, especially mayonnaise-based ones.

1 to 2 eggs
Parsley, chopped fine
Paprika, for dusting

● Hard-cook one or two eggs (see page 12), starting them off in cold water and allowing them 10 minutes boiling time. Cool rapidly, shell, and separate yolk from white. Pass the yolk through a metal sieve, pressing with a wooden spoon.

● Finely chop the egg white and either leave plain or mix with parsley. Use fine lines of alternating yolk and the speckled green egg whites.

● The parsley can be used as a third color, with the plain egg yolk and egg white, or the white can be dusted with paprika.

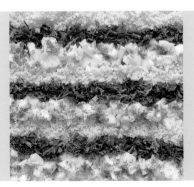

Decorating Ideas

- *Warm the shredded crêpes and serve as a garnish for light soups and consommés or add to a bowl of fresh noodles with sprigs of cilantro.*
- *The chopped egg garni can be used as a dressing for crab, fish and flans, mousses, salads and rice dishes, and mayonnaise-based dishes.*

31

Egg Flowers

The quantity of these ingredients varies according to the number of flowers you plan to make as a garnish.

1 to 2 eggs
Blanched cucumber peel
Chive stems and herb leaves

● Hard-cook one or two eggs (see page 12), then plunge into cold water immediately. Using an egg slicer or stainless steel knife, slice or halve the egg according to the required garnish. The whites can be molded into fancy shapes using pastry cutters or piping tube nozzles as cutters.

● Use sieved egg yolk to make the flower centers or cut out a round of yolk using a small plain piping nozzle as a cutter. Cucumber peel can be used for bolder stem and leaf shapes. Chive stems and herb leaves will produce a more delicate garnish.

Garnishing Ideas

Use these simple and delicious egg garnishes to add a creative touch to:

* *Terrines, pâtés, and mousses*
* *Cold meats and pies*
* *Aspic-coated dishes*

Smoked Fish Mayonnaise & Garlic Toast

These tasty bites are served Spanish club sandwich style. Serve them with a selection of other tapas dishes for a light supper.

SERVES **4** TO **6**

4 Tbsp olive oil

2 green bell peppers, seeded and cut into thin strips

Ground black pepper

I tomato, peeled and chopped

½ lb smoked mackerel, skinned and boned

½ lb smoked cod, skinned and boned

8 Tbsp garlic mayonnaise (see below)

6 slices of bread or I French loaf

I tsp garlic, crushed

2 Tbsp olive oil

GARLIC MAYONNAISE

Add 2 tsp crushed garlic to 1½ cups mayonnaise (see pages 4 and 62). Mix in a food processor or by hand.

● Heat the oil in a skillet and sauté the peppers over low heat. Add black pepper and the tomato. Cover and sauté for 20 minutes. Let cool.

● Mix the smoked fish with the garlic mayonnaise and black pepper until heavy cream consistency; add more garlic mayonnaise if necessary. Cut the bread into triangles or rounds; toast lightly. Brush on both sides with garlic and olive oil. Preheat the oven to 425°F and bake until golden, about 3 to 5 minutes.

● To serve, spoon a little of the pepper mixture over each toast piece. Spoon some of the fish mixture onto the peppers and serve immediately.

Green-Bean Frittatas

Tender young green beans, cooked in a flat omelet and topped with black-olive paste, make a delicious antipasto dish.

SERVES **4**

1 cup thin or extra-fine green beans
3 garlic cloves, minced
3 to 4 Tbsp extra virgin olive oil
Salt and ground black pepper
6 eggs, lightly beaten
3 Tbsp olive paste, such as tapenade
2 Tbsp thinly torn basil

● Steam or blanch the green beans until bright green and crisp-tender. Rinse in cold water, strain, and cut into bite-sized lengths.

● Warm the garlic and about 1 tablespoon olive oil in a skillet. Add the beans and warm through. Season. Remove the beans from the skillet and place them in a bowl with the eggs, stirring to mix well. In the same skillet, heat a tablespoon or so of the olive oil. When hot (not smoking), add a quarter of the bean–egg mixture, pouring and spreading it to form a flat omelet. Cook over medium heat until the base is golden, then brown on top under the broiler. Remove and place on a baking sheet. Repeat to make four omelets.

● To serve, spread each omelet with olive paste and sprinkle with basil.

Serving Idea

• *These frittatas are great picnic food. Serve with a crisp, fresh Mediterranean-style salad and a selection of other tapas dishes.*

Fried Squid

Make sure the squid is thoroughly cleaned prior to cooking. Follow the instructions given here or have your fish retailer clean the squid.

SERVES **4** TO **6**

2 lb squid, cleaned (see below)
3 eggs, beaten
Salt and ground black pepper
Flour
Oil, for deep-frying
Lemon wedges, to serve

● Place the squid in a large bowl and pour over the beaten eggs. Mix the two ingredients together well with your hands. Season and slowly mix in enough flour to form a thick paste around the squid.

● Heat a deep-fryer to 365°F and carefully add the squid piece by piece, in batches, into the oil. Shake and fry to a golden color. Remove the squid and drain on paper towels. Season and serve immediately with lemon wedges.

Cleaning Squid

- *Cut off the legs just below the eyes and keep to one side. Squeeze the top of the legs and the beak will pop out; discard. Empty the body sac over the sink by thrusting your fingers under the plastic-like backbone. Pull out the backbone; discard, then pull the innards out carefully in one piece; discard. Rinse the inside of the sac. Remove the fins firmly from where they join the body. The purple membraneous skin will then easily peel away. Rinse well and slice the body across into 1/2-inch rings.*
- *Rinse the rings and the legs again under cold water. Fill a heavy saucepan with water (enough to cover the squid), bring to a boil, then blanch the squid for 1 minute. Remove and let cool immediately under cold water.*

BRUNCH TIME

Raisin & Honey Bread

*This loaf contains a high proportion of yogurt, which gives it a
light, white center.*

SERVES 16

2¼ cups all-purpose flour
1½ tsp baking powder
½ tsp baking soda
½ tsp salt
1¾ cups plain yogurt
2 egg whites (see page 15)
⅓ cup raisins
2 Tbsp honey
Butter, for greasing

● Preheat an oven to 425°F. Mix the flour, baking powder, baking soda, and salt together in a large bowl. In a separate bowl, whisk together the yogurt and egg whites, then fold this into the flour mixture with the raisins and honey.

● Grease a 2 lb loaf pan and spoon in the mixture. Bake in the oven for 20 minutes until golden. Cool slightly and turn out of the pan. Serve warm.

Serving Idea

• *This delicious bread is low in fat. For a healthy breakfast serve with a selection of
  fresh fruit pieces and juices.*

Tunisian Scrambled Eggs

Spicy sausages flavor this piquant dish of scrambled eggs.

SERVES **4**

6 to 8 oz spicy sausages, such as chorizo, sliced

1 onion, thinly sliced

1 green and 1 red bell pepper, seeded and thinly sliced

4 to 5 Tbsp extra virgin olive oil

5 garlic cloves, chopped

5 ripe tomatoes, chopped or diced including
   their juices

6 eggs, lightly beaten

¼ tsp cumin

Salt and ground black pepper

¼ to 1 fresh green chili pepper, seeded and chopped

2 Tbsp chopped cilantro

Crusty fresh bread, to serve

Cook the sausages in an ungreased skillet until lightly browned. Pour off any excess fat and drain on a plate. Sauté the onion and bell peppers in olive olive until softened. Stir in the garlic and cook through for a few minutes. Add the tomatoes. Increase the heat and cook over medium high heat until the sauce thickens, about 8 minutes.

Pour in the eggs, sprinkle with cumin, seasoning, and chili. Cook over low to medium heat, stirring occasionally with a wooden spoon until the eggs are no longer runny.

Sprinkle the mixture with cilantro and serve immediately with fresh bread.

Rolled Omelet

Fried in fragrant olive oil, this delicious omelet has a tangy, fresh filling of goat cheese.

SERVES **4**

8 eggs, lightly beaten (allow 2 eggs per person)

2 to 3 Tbsp milk

Salt and ground black pepper

4 to 5 Tbsp extra virgin olive oil

½ green chili, chopped fine

2 garlic cloves, chopped fine

4 to 6 oz goat cheese

3 Tbsp chopped dill

3 Tbsp chopped cilantro

Sour cream, to serve (optional)

● Prepare four individual omelets by mixing two eggs with a little milk for each omelet. Season to taste. Pour a tablespoon or two of olive oil into the omelet pan and warm, but don't overheat it (it should be almost smoking, but not quite).

● Pour in the required amount of beaten egg. Cook for a few minutes over low heat, lifting the edges from the sides, and letting the runny egg flow underneath. When the egg is nearly set, sprinkle in the chili, garlic, goat cheese, dill, and cilantro; fold over.

● Roll the omelet out of the pan and serve hot, topped with sour cream, if desired.

Ham 'n' Egg Cocottes

These popular favorites are perfect as an appetizer or for a special breakfast or brunch.

SERVES **4**

¼ cup ham, cut into strips
⅛ stick butter
1½ cups button mushrooms, wiped and sliced
Ground black pepper
4 medium eggs
4 Tbsp heavy cream
¾ cup Brie, cubed
Warm, crusty bread, to serve

● Preheat an oven to 375°F for 10 minutes prior to baking the cocottes. Line four ramekin dishes with the ham. Melt the butter in a small skillet and gently sauté the mushrooms for 2 minutes. Drain on paper towels and place in the ramekin dishes. Season with black pepper.

● Break an egg into each dish, then pour over 1 tablespoon cream. Dot with the cheese. Place in a roasting pan half-filled with boiling water (*bain marie*), then bake for 15 to 20 minutes or until set, as liked. Serve with bread.

Serving Ideas

- Use three skinned, seeded, and chopped tomatoes in place of the mushrooms. Sauté gently for 1 minute.
- Try one small onion, chopped fine and sautéed for 4 to 5 minutes or until softened instead of the mushrooms.
- Shredded Gruyère cheese can be used in place of Brie.

Vitality Shake

This delicious drink is a good energy provider.

MAKES ABOUT **2** CUPS

1¼ cups skim milk

⅔ cup plain yogurt

1 small egg (see page 4)

1 to 2 tsp powdered Brewers' yeast

1 to 2 tsp clear honey

½ tsp grated nutmeg, plus extra for dusting

2 tsp wheat germ

● Place the milk, yogurt, egg, yeast, honey, and nutmeg in a blender and mix together. Pour into a serving glass. Sprinkle with wheat germ, then dust with more nutmeg to serve.

Berry Sherbet

The perfect summer refreshment. Blending produces the best results. It can be garnished with berries skewered onto toothpicks, if desired.

MAKES ABOUT 2¼ CUPS

MIXED BERRY JUICE
1 cup strawberries
½ cup raspberries
½ cup blueberries
½ cup blackberries

1 medium egg white (see pages 4 and 15)
1 quantity Mixed Berry Juice (see above)
Ice cubes
1 tsp clear honey (optional)

● To make the mixed berry juice, wash and hull the fruits, setting aside a few berries for decoration, if desired. Blend all the remaining fruits together, transfer to a jug, and set aside.

● Whisk the egg white until thick and frothy, but not stiff. Pour the juice into a blender, add a few ice cubes, and the egg white. Blend for a few seconds until slushy and foaming. Taste and sweeten with honey, if liked. Pour into a glass and serve immediately.

Cheesy Bacon Muffins

These muffins are delicious as a brunch dish or with scrambled eggs. Serve with cream cheese flavored with snipped fresh herbs, if desired.

MAKES 12

Vegetable oil
6 slices bacon
1½ cups all-purpose flour
2 tsp baking powder
½ tsp salt

2 tsp sugar
1 cup Swiss cheese, shredded
3 to 4 scallions, chopped fine
1 egg
¾ cup milk
1 Tbsp Dijon mustard
Flavored cream cheese spread, to serve (optional)

● Preheat the oven to 400°F. Grease or spray 12 one-cup muffin tins, or line each tin with paper cases. Put the bacon in a large skillet and fry over medium heat, turning once, until crisp and brown on both sides. Drain on paper towels and pour the remaining fat into a cup. Add extra oil, if necessary, to make 4 tablespoons. When cool, crumble the bacon into small pieces.

● Meanwhile, sift the flour, baking powder, and salt into a large bowl. Stir in the sugar, cheese, and scallions, tossing lightly to mix. Add the bacon and mix again, then make a well in the center.

● Beat the egg with the milk in another bowl until well blended. Then beat in the mustard and reserved bacon fat. Pour into the well and stir lightly until just combined. Do not overmix; the batter should be slightly lumpy.

● Spoon the mixture into the prepared muffin cups and bake until risen, golden, and springy when pressed, 15 to 20 minutes. Set the pan on a wire rack to cool, about 2 minutes, then remove the muffins to the rack to cool until just warm. Serve with cream cheese spread or as liked.

CLASSIC EGGS

Eggs Florentine

This is a popular breakfast, brunch, or supper dish.

SERVES **8**

8 medium eggs
1 lb fresh spinach, tough stalks discarded
   and well washed
4 Tbsp butter
1 small onion, chopped fine
1 to 2 garlic cloves, crushed
⅓ cup all-purpose flour
1 cup milk
1 tsp Dijon mustard
Salt and ground black pepper
¼ cup Gruyère cheese, shredded
Warm, crusty bread, to serve

● Place the eggs in a heavy saucepan, cover with cold water, and bring to a boil. Boil gently for 10 minutes, then plunge into cold water. Leave until cool. Peel and cut in half.

● Meanwhile, place the spinach with water just clinging to the leaves in a heavy saucepan. Cover with a lid and cook for 3 to 4 minutes. Drain and chop fine. Heat 1 tablespoon of the butter in a small skillet. Gently sauté the onion and garlic for 5 minutes or until softened. Stir in the spinach, then place in the base of an ovenproof gratin dish. Place the boiled egg halves on top.

● Melt the remaining butter in a small heavy saucepan. Stir in the flour and cook for 2 minutes. Remove from the heat and gradually stir in the milk. Return to the heat and cook, stirring, until the mixture thickens and coats the back of a wooden spoon. Remove from the heat and stir in the mustard, seasoning, and half the cheese.

● To serve, preheat broiler to medium. Pour the sauce over the eggs. Sprinkle with the remaining cheese and place under the broiler for 8 to 10 minutes, or until golden brown and bubbly. Serve immediately with warm, crusty bread.

Spanish Tortilla

Serve the tortilla in wedges as a tapas with drinks or as a light appetizer or picnic dish.

MAKES 1

3 potatoes
Salt and ground black pepper
3 Tbsp olive oil
1 onion, chopped fine or sliced
3 eggs, beaten
Chopped chives, to garnish

● Slice the potatoes very finely and place them in a heavy saucepan of cold, salted water. Bring to a boil and parboil for 5 minutes.

● Place a skillet over low heat and heat the oil. Add the onion and potato slices. Shake the skillet and stir to prevent the mixture sticking to the base. Season lightly with salt and pepper. Reduce the heat slightly and cook, tossing the mixture until golden brown. Season the eggs and stir in the mixture from the skillet.

● Replace the skillet over the heat and when hot, pour the tortilla mixture into it. It will seal immediately. Cook for 2 minutes, then place a large plate over the omelet, flip it onto the plate and then slide it back into the skillet so that the uncooked side is now over the heat. Cook for 1 minute.

● Let cool, garnish with chives, and slice to serve. The omelet should be thick, firm, and cake-like, unlike a French omelet.

Tip

• *Many ingredients and flavorings may be used (or used up!) in tortillas, for instance green bell peppers (sliced and added to the onion), mushrooms, cooked ham, cheese, and so on.*

Spaghetti Carbonara

This rich cream sauce is the ultimate Italian classic.

MAKES I CUP

2 Tbsp unsalted butter

3 Tbsp olive oil

2 to 3 garlic cloves, crushed

I large onion, chopped fine

4 oz pancetta

2 medium egg yolks (see pages 4 and 15)

⅔ cup light whipping cream

4 Tbsp freshly shredded Parmesan cheese

Salt and ground black pepper

I lb fresh pasta, freshly shredded Parmesan cheese,
   and parsley, chopped fine, to serve

● Heat the butter and oil in a skillet and gently sauté the garlic and onion for 5 minutes, or until softened but not browned. Add the pancetta and continue to sauté for another 2 minutes.

● Meanwhile, beat the egg yolks with the cream and Parmesan cheese; season and reserve. Cook the pasta in plenty of salted boiling water until *al dente*, about I to 2 minutes. Drain and return to the saucepan. Add the onion/pancetta mixture; heat through for 2 minutes, stirring occasionally, then remove from the heat.

● Add the egg and cream mixture. Quickly mix together with two forks so that the eggs are cooked in the heat of the pasta. Season and serve immediately with additional Parmesan and parsley.

Spaghetti Carbonara

Quiche Lorraine

This recipe originates from the Lorraine region of France, where it is served as an appetizer.

SERVES **4** TO **6**

9-in tart pan lined with shortcrust pastry, partially
  baked blind
8 oz bacon, cut into ½-in slices
1½ cups heavy cream
3 eggs
1 egg yolk (see page 15)
½ tsp salt
Ground black pepper
Freshly grated nutmeg
5½ oz shredded Gruyère (optional)

● Preheat the oven to 375°F. Set the tart case on a baking sheet for easier handling.

● Place the bacon in a skillet over low heat. When the fat begins to melt, increase the heat to medium, and fry, stirring occasionally, until crisp. Drain on paper towels, then sprinkle over the base of the tart case.

● In a bowl, blend the cream and eggs together well. Season and add a little nutmeg. Stir in the cheese, if using. Pour the mixture into the tart case. Bake until the filling is set and golden, about 35 minutes. Transfer to a cooling rack and serve at room temperature.

Salade Niçoise

*This fabulous salad from France makes a refreshing lunch or dinner
on a warm day.*

SERVES **4** TO **6**

1 small head lettuce
¾ cup French vinaigrette
2 cups green beans, cooked
2 cups cooked potatoes, diced
8-oz can tuna, drained and flaked
2 to 3 tomatoes, peeled and quartered
2 hard-cooked eggs, quartered (see page 12)
6 anchovies, cut in half
1 Tbsp chopped tarragon, chervil, or parsley

● Wash and dry the lettuce, tear it into small pieces, and place in a salad bowl. Sprinkle a few tablespoons of dressing over the top.

● Arrange the beans, potatoes, and tuna on top of the salad greens, and place the tomatoes around the edge of the bowl. Top with eggs and anchovies. Pour over the remaining dressing, sprinkle with herbs, and serve immediately.

French Vinaigrette

If you want to make your own vinaigrette, this recipe is simple but very tasty.

MAKES ABOUT **1** CUP

½ tsp salt
⅛ tsp freshly ground pepper
¼ cup vinegar or lemon juice
¼ to ½ tsp Dijon-style mustard
¾ cup walnut or olive oil

Whisk together the salt, pepper, vinegar or lemon juice, mustard, and walnut or olive oil in a nonreactive medium-size bowl until well combined. The dressing will keep for about 3 days in the refrigerator.

Omelet Fines Herbes

Packed with nutrients, this omelet is a classic French dish.

SERVES 1

2 medium eggs
Salt and ground black pepper
1 Tbsp chopped herbs (try parsley, chervil, tarragon, and chives)
1 Tbsp water
1 Tbsp unsalted butter

● Lightly whisk the eggs with the seasoning to taste until frothy. Stir in the herbs and water.

● Melt the butter in a skillet, tilting the skillet to coat the base evenly. Pour in the beaten eggs; stir gently with a fork, drawing the mixture from the sides of the skillet to the center. When the egg has set, stop stirring, and cook for a further minute. Then, with a palette knife, fold over a third of the omelet to the center, then fold over the opposite side.

● To serve, gently slide the omelet onto a warmed plate and serve immediately.

Ideas for Alternative Fillings

- *Try stirring ¼ cup shredded cheese into the eggs when the base has set, or ¾ cup mushrooms, sliced and sautéed.*
- *¼ cup shredded ham makes a good filling, or two tomatoes, skinned and seeded, then chopped. Also, 1 cup cooked, peeled shrimp.*
- *Place mushrooms, ham, tomatoes, and shrimp in the center of the omelet once set. Cook for 1 to 2 minutes to heat through. Fold over and serve immediately, sprinkled with parsley, chopped fine.*

Crab Louis

This salad was served at Solari's, a restaurant in San Francisco, as early as 1914.

SERVES **4**

½ head iceberg lettuce, shredded
2 cups flaked, fresh crabmeat
1 cup Mayonnaise (see pages 4 and 62)
⅓ cup whipped cream
2 tsp Worcestershire sauce
1 tsp chopped dill
2 to 3 Tbsp chili sauce
2 to 3 Tbsp shredded onion
¼ cup chopped green bell pepper
1 to 3 Tbsp chopped parsley
Cayenne pepper, to taste
3 to 4 hard-cooked eggs, quartered
3 to 4 tomatoes, cut into wedges
6 to 8 bottled artichoke hearts

● Divide the lettuce between four plates. Place one-quarter of the crabmeat on top of the lettuce on each plate. In a small bowl, mix the mayonnaise with the cream, Worcestershire sauce, dill, chili sauce, onion, bell pepper, and parsley. Add cayenne pepper to taste.

● To serve, spread one-quarter of the mixture liberally over the crabmeat on each plate. Top with eggs, tomato wedges, and artichoke hearts.

ON THE SIDE

Original Caesar Salad

Restaurateur Caesar Cardini invented this salad for Hollywood actors in the 1920s. Today, it is served in fine dining establishments the world over.

SERVES **4**

1 egg (see page 4)
¼ tsp salt
¼ tsp ground black pepper
2 Tbsp white wine vinegar
1 garlic clove, crushed
½ tsp Dijon mustard
1 tsp Worcestershire sauce
2 anchovies, chopped fine
2 Tbsp fresh lemon juice

½ cup extra virgin olive oil
1 head Romaine lettuce, rinsed, dried, and torn
   into bite-size pieces, chilled
¼ cup Parmesan cheese, freshly shredded
4 anchovy strips, to garnish

PARMESAN CROUTONS
1½ Tbsp olive oil
1 large garlic clove (left whole)
2 oz French or Italian-style bread, cubed
⅛ cup Parmesan cheese, freshly shredded

● Cook the egg in its shell in simmering water for 1½ minutes. Set aside until cool enough to handle. In a large bowl, combine the salt, pepper, vinegar, garlic, mustard, Worcestershire sauce, and anchovies. Break the egg into a small bowl and sprinkle lemon juice on top. Whisk until frothy and pour the mixture into the larger bowl with the anchovies and other ingredients. Continue whisking while gradually adding the olive oil.

● Make the croûtons by heating the oil and garlic in a heavy skillet until the garlic turns golden. Discard the garlic. Add the bread cubes and cook, stirring for 3 to 5 minutes until lightly browned; toss the cubes in the Parmesan cheese.

● Add the lettuce, cheese, and croûtons to the large bowl. Toss gently to coat the salad greens. Place anchovy strips artfully across the top of the bowl and serve immediately.

Mayonnaise

For best results, make this recipe in a food processor or blender.

MAKES ABOUT ¾ CUP

1 egg (see page 4)
1 tsp dry mustard
Pinch of cayenne pepper
1 tsp sugar
½ cup olive or vegetable oil
3 Tbsp lemon juice
Salt

Simple Flavored Mayonnaises

- *Add chopped fresh herbs, such as parsley, chives, and dill.*
- *Chop the leaves and fine stems of some watercress and add to the mixture.*
- *For caper mayonnaise, add some chopped capers and a dash of tarragon vinegar.*

● Combine the egg, dry mustard, cayenne pepper, sugar and ¼ cup oil. Process on high speed for 1 minute. Add lemon juice and blend on high again for 10 seconds. Turn the food processor or blender to low, add the remaining oil, a little at a time, until thick. Add salt to taste, and serve or store in the refrigerator.

Green Goddess Dressing

Created in San Francisco, this dressing is named after a popular 1930s movie. It will keep for about three days in the refrigerator.

MAKES ABOUT **2** CUPS

1 cup mayonnaise (see pages 4 and 62)

1 garlic clove, chopped fine

3 anchovy fillets, drained on paper towels
    and chopped fine

4 Tbsp chives, chopped fine

4 Tbsp parsley, chopped fine

1 Tbsp lemon juice

1 Tbsp tarragon vinegar

½ cup sour cream

● Put all the ingredients into a medium bowl and stir together.

Waldorf Salad

This recipe was created by chef Oscar Tschirky in the 1890s for a party to celebrate the opening of the Waldorf-Astoria Hotel in New York.

SERVES **4**

1¼ cups diced tart apples

1¼ cups seedless grapes

2 Tbsp shredded coconut (optional)

½ cup dates, pitted and chopped (optional)

⅓ cup diced celery

⅔ cup Mayonnaise (see page 4 and 62)

1 Tbsp walnut oil

2 tsp fresh lemon or lime juice

1 tsp sugar

¼ tsp ground ginger

½ cup walnuts, chopped

● In a large bowl, mix together the apples, grapes, coconut (if using), dates (if using), and celery. In a separate bowl, whisk together the mayonnaise, walnut oil, lemon or lime juice, sugar, and ginger. Pour the mixture over the salad and lightly toss. Cover and refrigerate. Just before serving, gently mix in the walnuts.

Creamy Egg Dip

This delicious dip makes an ideal snack on weekends. Serve with sausages, bacon strips, bite-size pieces of smoked salmon, and tomato wedges.

MAKES ABOUT 1¼ CUPS

6 eggs
⅔ cup heavy cream
Salt and freshly ground black pepper
2 Tbsp butter
2 Tbsp chives, chopped

● Beat the eggs with the cream in a bowl. Season with salt and pepper.

● Melt the butter in a large (if possible, nonstick) skillet until it gently sizzles. Pour in the egg mixture and cook over a moderately low heat, stirring continuously, until cooked, about 6 to 7 minutes. The eggs should have a creamy, smooth, scrambled-egg appearance.

● Transfer the egg dip to a serving bowl and sprinkle with the chopped chives. Enjoy while warm.

Egg & Parsley Dip

This dip is great served with toasted strips of white and brown bread.

MAKES ABOUT 1¼ CUPS

3 hard-cooked eggs, chilled and shelled (see page 12)
⅔ cup Mayonnaise (see page 62)
1 Tbsp milk
5 Tbsp parsley, chopped fine
Freshly ground black pepper
Sprig of parsley

● Place the hard-cooked eggs in a bowl and, with the back of a fork, mash them into fine pieces.

● Stir the mayonnaise and milk thoroughly into the eggs. Add the parsley and season well with freshly ground black pepper. Cover and chill.

● Spoon the dip into a serving bowl and garnish with a sprig of parsley.

Russian Salad

A fresh vegetable salad that can be served as a tapas or light snack.

SERVES **4** TO **6**

8 medium potatoes, peeled
1 medium carrot, diced
1 cup fresh peas
2 hard-cooked eggs (see page 12), cooled, peeled, and cubed
7-oz can tuna in unsalted water, drained and flaked
1 red bell pepper, seeded and diced
½ cup corn
¼ cup black olives, pitted
1½ cups Mayonnaise (see pages 4 and 62)

● Put the potatoes in a heavy saucepan of water and bring to a boil. Cover, lower the heat, and simmer for about 20 to 25 minutes or until cooked. Drain, cool, and cut into ¼-inch cubes.

● Boil the carrot and peas for 3 to 5 minutes until lightly cooked. Drain. Mix the potatoes with the egg, tuna, carrot, peas, pepper, corn, and olives in a large salad bowl.

● Just before serving, add the mayonnaise to the salad and toss to coat.

Russian Salad

Aioli

Aioli is a type of mayonnaise that has puréed garlic cloves as a base. It originates from Provence.

MAKES ABOUT 1 ½ CUPS

6 to 12 garlic cloves
Salt and ground black pepper
2 egg yolks (see pages 4 and 15)
½ to 1 tsp Dijon mustard
About 1 ¼ cups olive oil
1 ½ Tbsp lemon juice or white wine vinegar

● Place the garlic and a dash of salt in a mortar or bowl and crush them together until reduced to a paste. Work in the egg yolks and the mustard.

● Add the oil, a few drops at a time, while stirring slowly, evenly, and constantly. After half the oil has been incorporated, add half the lemon juice or white wine vinegar. The rest of the oil can now be added a little more quickly, but the sauce must be stirred in the same way.

● Finally, add the remaining lemon juice or vinegar and season.

Zesty Asparagus Salad

The slight sharpness of the mustard in this salad accents the delicate flavor of the asparagus. To save time, the vinaigrette may be made up to two days in advance.

SERVES **4**

1 lb asparagus, trimmed

4 to 8 large lettuce leaves

1 hard-cooked egg, chopped fine (see page 12)

ZESTY VINAIGRETTE

¾ cup mild olive oil

2 Tbsp red wine vinegar

2 tsp Dijon mustard

¼ tsp black pepper

⅛ tsp salt

1 large garlic clove, crushed

2 Tbsp snipped chives

● Soak the asparagus stalks in cold water to remove any dirt, then drain. Bring a large, shallow saucepan of water to a boil, add the asparagus, and cook for 5 to 7 minutes until tender-crisp. Remove each stalk with tongs; drain and rinse immediately under cold running water. Drain again, wrap in paper towels, and chill in the refrigerator for about 2 hours.

● Prepare the vinaigrette. Place the oil, vinegar, mustard, pepper, salt, garlic, and chives in a jar with a secure lid. Shake until thoroughly blended. Refrigerate for 2 hours before using.

● To serve, line each of four plates with 1 to 2 lettuce leaves. Divide the chilled asparagus between plates and spoon 1 tablespoon of vinaigrette on each plate. Sprinkle the salads with hard-cooked egg and serve immediately.

SOMETHING SWEET

Fresh Fruit Brûlée

Experiment with different fruits and berries in this delicious dessert.

SERVES **4** TO **6**

6 oz fresh raspberries

6 oz fresh strawberries, sliced

4 oz fresh redcurrants, stringed

2 egg yolks (see page 15)

2 Tbsp cornstarch

¼ cup superfine sugar

½ pt milk

1¼ cups heavy cream

About ¾ cup raw brown sugar

● Place the fruit in either a flameproof dish or individual ramekin dishes. Beat together the egg yolks, cornstarch, and sugar. Heat the milk until almost boiling, pour over the egg mixture and return to a clean pan. Cook over a very low heat, stirring, until custard thickens. Allow to cool completely. Whip the cream until fairly thick and fold into the custard mixture. Use it to cover the fruit evenly. Sprinkle over the raw brown sugar to cover the custard completely; chill well.

● Just before serving, preheat a broiler and place the dish or dishes underneath to lightly melt and caramelize the sugar. Serve immediately.

Vanilla Pod Gelato

An ice cream classic that is delicious served on its own or as an accompaniment to all kinds of desserts.

SERVES **4** TO **6**

1 large vanilla pod
2½ cups milk
⅓ cup superfine sugar
6 large egg yolks, beaten (see pages 4 and 15)
½ tsp vanilla extract (optional)

Carefully split open the vanilla pod with a sharp knife and scrape out the seeds, reserving them for later use. Heat the pod in the milk with the sugar, stirring until dissolved.

Beat the egg yolks until slightly thickened and pale in color, then pour on the hot milk, beating constantly. Rinse the heavy saucepan with cold water, return the mixture to it, and heat gently. Stir constantly, until the mixture has thickened sufficiently to just coat the back of a wooden spoon. Remove from the heat, stir in the reserved vanilla seeds, then allow the custard to cool completely.

Remove the vanilla pod (rinse and store for later use), and taste the custard; it should have a really strong vanilla flavor. Add up to half a teaspoon vanilla extract, if necessary, to emphasize the vanilla. Turn the mixture into an ice-cream machine, and freeze-churn until ready to serve.

Serving Ideas

- *Fresh fruits, such as strawberries and raspberries.*
- *Banana Split—cut the banana in half lengthwise, top with the ice cream, flavored syrups, whipped cream, and a maraschino cherry.*
- *Warm apple pie.*

Sweet Whiskey Omelet

A sweet variation on the traditional omelet.

SERVES **2**

3 eggs, separated (see page 15)

1 Tbsp butter

1 Tbsp superfine sugar

2 Tbsp whiskey

2 Tbsp Cointreau

2 tsp sifted confectioner's sugar

Whisk the egg yolks until creamy and, in a separate bowl, whisk the whites until stiff. Fold the yolks into the whites. Melt the butter in a skillet and pour in the mixture. Cook gently for 5 minutes. Place under a preheated broiler for 2 to 3 minutes or until set. Sprinkle with sugar and liquor. Heat for 1 to 2 minutes. Scatter confectioner's sugar over the top of the omelet and serve immediately.

Zabaglione

This egg-based dessert comes from Italy and is served warm in tall glasses.

SERVES **4**

4 egg yolks (see pages 4 and 15)
3 Tbsp superfine sugar
5 fl oz Marsala wine
Sponge fingers, to serve

● Place the egg yolks, sugar, and Marsala wine in a heatproof basin, placed over a heavy saucepan of gently simmering water. Whisk until very thick and frothy. Spoon into warm glasses and serve immediately with the sponge fingers.

Serving Idea

- *This warm frothy dessert can also be served as a sauce over cakes, fresh fruit pieces, ice creams, and pastries.*

Mile-High Ice-Cream Pie

As the meringue for this dessert is frozen, the whole thing may be prepared several days in advance. If you really want to impress your guests, you may like to fill the cookie case with a double quantity of ice cream or frozen yogurt. If so, increase the meringue ingredients to 4 egg whites and 1¼ cups superfine sugar, and double the amount of fruit.

SERVES **6** TO **8**

½ cup butter
2 cups crushed chocolate-covered graham crackers
1 tsp superfine sugar
1½ cups strawberries or raspberries,
   roughly chopped

Good-quality purchased strawberry ice cream or
   raspberry frozen yogurt
2 large egg whites (see pages 4 and 15)
Pinch of salt
⅔ cup superfine sugar
1 tsp cream of tartar

● Melt the butter, then stir in the crushed crackers and sugar; mix thoroughly. Press into an 8-inch ovenproof ceramic dish and leave to chill in the refrigerator (about 1 hour).

● Mix the fruit into the ice cream or frozen yogurt (allow the ice cream to soften for about 5 minutes first), then pack it into the cookie base, mounding it up in the center. Harden the pie in the freezer for 1 to 1½ hours.

● Preheat an oven (not the broiler) to its hottest setting. Whisk the egg whites with the salt until stiff, then gradually add the sugar and cream of tartar, whisking all the time, until the meringue is stiff and glossy. Do not overbeat the egg whites once you have added the sugar.

● Pile the meringue over the hardened ice cream, ensuring that it is completely covered and that the meringue meets the base all around the pie. Bake for 4 to 5 minutes, until the meringue is lightly browned.

● Leave the ice cream pie for 5 to 10 minutes until cool, then return to the freezer for a further 2 to 3 hours, until the meringue is firm. Remove the pie from the freezer about 20 minutes before serving, and serve in slices.

Caramel Ice Cream

Serve this ice cream in tall glasses, spiked with shards of caramel. The flavor is subtle, so do not serve it after a highly spiced main course.

SERVES **4** TO **6**

½ cup superfine sugar
2½ cups light cream
3 large egg yolks, beaten (see pages 4 and 15)
⅔ cup heavy cream, beaten until thick and floppy

● Heat the sugar very slowly in a heavy saucepan until dissolved, then increase the heat and bring the syrup to a boil. Continue cooking, without stirring, until the mixture turns a rich chestnut brown.

● Meanwhile, heat the light cream gently until almost boiling, then take it off the heat (this is important) and beat in the hot caramel. If the cream is not hot enough, the caramel will spit and form into balls in the mixture. Allow the caramel cream to cool completely.

● Stir the beaten egg yolks into the chilled mixture with the heavy cream, then freeze-churn until ready to serve.

Caramel Shards

• *The shards can be made up in advance and stored on waxed paper until needed. Make up an extra quantity of caramel (see method). With a teaspoon, drizzle caramel onto waxed paper in shard shapes (see photograph). Allow to set, then peel the paper away from the shards.*

Café au Lait Gelato

An intensely flavored Italian-style ice cream. Serve in scoops in sugared cornet wafers, with whipped cream or a dollop of mascarpone.

SERVES **6**

2½ cups whole milk
⅓ cup instant espresso
½ cup superfine sugar, or more according to taste
6 egg yolks, beaten (see pages 4 and 15)

● Heat the milk in a heavy saucepan with the instant espresso and sugar, stirring until the sugar has dissolved.

● Beat the egg yolks in a bowl until pale, then pour on the hot milk, stirring constantly. Rinse the saucepan, return the custard to the pan, and heat gently, stirring constantly, until the mixture has thickened just enough to coat the back of a wooden spoon. Pour the custard into a clean bowl and let cool completely. Chill for 1 hour.

● Scrape the custard into an ice cream machine and freeze-churn until ready to serve.

Index